Tomáš Špidlík

The art of purifying the heart

Translated by Liam Kelly

CONVIVIUMPRESS

SERIES SAPIENTIA

2 0 1 0

The art of purifying the heart

Original Title: *L'arte di purificare il cuore*
by Tomáš Špidlík
© LIPA S.R.L.

© Convivium Press 2010.
All rights reserved
Todos los derechos reservados.
For the English Edition.

http://www.conviviumpress.com
sales@conviviumpress.com
convivium@conviviumpress.com

7661 NW 68th St, Suite 108,
Miami, Florida 33166. USA.
Phone: +1 (786) 8669718

Edited *by* Rafael Luciani
Translated *by* Liam Kelly
Designed *by* Eduardo Chumaceiro d'E
Series: *Sapientia*

ISBN: 978-1-934996-18-8

Printed in Colombia
Impreso en Colombia
D'VINNI, S.A.

Convivium Press
Miami, 2010

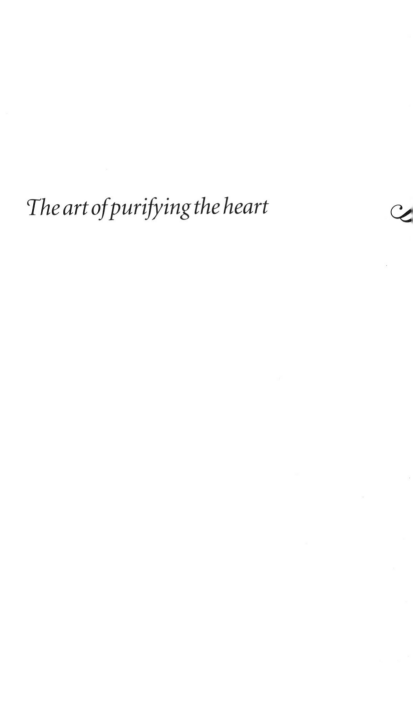

The art of purifying the heart

Contents

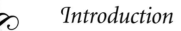 *Introduction*

Let us begin with some representative texts:

«*This is the covenant I shall make with the House of Israel when those days have come, Yahweh declares. Within them I shall plant my Law, writing it on their hearts*» (Jer 31:33).

«*...so that Christ may live in your hearts through faith, and then, planted in love and built on love, with all God's holy people you will have the strength to grasp the breadth and the length, the height and the depth; so that, knowing the love of Christ, which is beyond knowledge, you may be filled with the utter fullness of God*» (Eph 3:17-19).

«*If we take great trouble over this, then maybe the air we feel around us will not be as close to our exterior sense as is the Spirit of God who is continuously in our hearts. Through him the memory of him is clear at every moment, and in this way he dwells all the more in us...*» (*Martyrius Sahdônâ, 7th century Syriac writer*).

«*The truly pure of heart are those who despise earthly things and seek the things of heaven, and who never cease to adore and behold the Lord God living and true with a pure heart and soul*» (*Saint Francis of Assisi*).

«*It is not the richness of science which satisfies the soul, but feeling and tasting things from within*» (*Saint Ignatius of Loyola*).

«*Our heart is truly the root and center of life. It reveals if a person's state is good or evil and incites the other forces to action and, after they have carried out their work, it receives within itself the results of these actions to strengthen or weaken that feeling which characterizes a person's permanent disposition. It seems, therefore, that controlling life should be conceded to the heart —and in fact that is so in many people and to a lesser degree in many others— and perhaps initially it was thus. But* passions came and disturbed everything. When they are present, our heart is not a sure sentinel, our impressions are not as they should be, tastes are perverse and lead the activity of the other forces to dissipation. The plan, therefore, is this: keep the heart under control and submit all sentiments, tastes and inclinations to a severe evaluation. When it is purified from passions, then it will be able to act at its own convenience» (Theophan the Recluse, Russian spiritual writer, † 1894).

«If religion is a personal relationship with God, then contact with the Divinity is only possible in the depths of my «I», in the depths of the heart, because God, as Pascal says, is sensitive to the heart» (B. Vyšeslavcev, Russian theologian, † 1954).

The mystery of good and evil

1
What is the source of evil?

This is a question that people have continually asked, even while remaining ever convinced that the problem of evil sets before us a mystery. Schematically, prior to Christianity we can distinguish three different fundamental answers to such a question:

That of cosmic dualism: there are two types of forces in the world which fight against each other: those of the good divinities and those of the evil divinities, the light and the darkness. Good appears stronger, but the struggle against evil is eternal.

That of anthropological dualism: good and evil are within the human person. Their struggle manifests itself as the opposition between the flesh and the spirit. The desires of the flesh lead us to evil, the spirit raises us on high. But by ascesis man can weaken the influence of the flesh and thus strengthen the spirit.

That of moral dualism: it is not the flesh in itself which leads to evil, but the «passions». So virtue consists in overcoming the passions and living according to reason.

2
Can the explanation of cosmic dualism be accepted?

This idea, typical of ancient eastern religions, is reflected in the fables that are like the oldest documents of human literature. These fables contain good fairies, evil witches and princes who fight dragons. Children listen willingly to these tales because there is a clear distinction in them between what is good and what is evil and at the end faith is manifested in the victory of good. And yet, deep down, this conception contradicts Christian revelation. Everything that exists was created by God and everything that God has created is good. Therefore the existence of a force of evil independent from God, parallel to him, cannot be admitted, and nor can the existence of a being evil by nature from the very start.

3

But, as Saint Paul attests (Cf. ROM 7), sin is hidden in our flesh, the flesh opposes the spirit. How are we to understan this opposition?

In fact, in the Bible and in ascetical literature, the «flesh» is denoted as the source of evil. But this term should not lead us into error. «Flesh» does not mean the human body, but it is a term used in a moral sense, indicating the totality of temptations caused by sin which has already made its home in us. It is also called «concupiscence», of which it is said «it comes from sin, draws us to sin, but in itself it is not yet sin». Therefore it would be mistaken to think that our body, the material component of the human person, is evil. The body of Christ is holy and we are called to sanctify our body in union with Him.

4

Just like the ancient stoic philosophers, Christian morality, too, teaches about taming the passions; must these, then, be considered evil?

The term «passion» can be understood in two ways. Positively, it can be understood as a good, perceptible desire, when it indicates a natural inclination: for example the desire to eat when hungry, the joy of being on the move, the wish to get married at the right time, etc. Negatively, when passions overstep the mark and are difficult to control they lead us to evil.

But not even the passions in themselves constitute sin. Through God's grace, the human person usually possesses freedom and the strength to overcome the inclinations to evil. And if, to stretch a point, the passion were to be so strong that someone would lose their freedom or knowledge of good or evil, he/she would commit, as the moralists say, a sin «materially», but before God such a sin would be accounted for due to the person's extreme weakness.

5

So, according to Christian teaching, what must be considered «evil» and who is responsible for it coming in to the world?

Only sin is truly evil, that is the fruit of a human person's free consent to the evil. Therefore, only the human person is responsible for the evil which takes over his/her heart and through him/her enters into the world. The Church Fathers wrote homilies on the theme «God is not the cause of evil» (Saint Basil). They harangued people with these words: «Do not blame God nor the devil, nor the world, nor the flesh with its passions, but blame yourself and only yourself!» Saint John Chrysostom wrote a treatise entitled: *No one can harm the man who does not injure himself.* Does it seem a sad observation? Is it? In a certain sense, yes, but there is also the other side of the coin: if on the one hand we ourselves have caused evil, on the other we ourselves can try to remedy it.

6

But in the world we encounter so many problems that we feel are not our fault!

The Fathers distinguished between the so-called «physical» evils and the «moral» ones. Moral evil is the sin. Physical evils are sickness, death, natural disasters, plague, etc. Even their distant origin is in sin, which goes back to the first disobedi-ence of Adam. Physical evil has a punitive character. And it is precisely because of this that they work for good: if accepted in a spirit of penitence. Suffering puts us on guard against seeking our definitive happiness in the world in order to turn our minds to God.

Chapter 2

The serpent in the heart's paradise

1

Where is the origin of sin to be found? How should the biblical account of the serpent in Paradise be interpreted?

Gen 3 tells the story of the first sin: the temptation to eat the forbidden fruit, the conversation between Eve and the seductive serpent, Adam's consent, the banishment from paradise. The Fathers believed that the experience of each person confirmed and extended in history what *Genesis* recounted in the early chapters. Each of us possesses a paradise, that is the heart created by God in a peaceful state. And each of us lives the experience of the serpent, which penetrates into the heart to seduce us. The serpent takes the shape of an evil thought. Origen, and many other Fathers agreed, wrote that «the source and beginning of each sin is the thought» (in Greek *logismos*).

2

How can a simple thought cause evil?

It is not a simple thought, but an impure, evil thought. To be quite honest, what we often call temptations are not even real thoughts, but rather images of the fantasy to which is added the suggestion of carrying out something evil. Saint Maximus the Confessor illustrated this situation with examples taken from daily life, stating, for example, that the capacity to think, and not even the thought is evil. Woman is not evil. Nor is it evil to think of a woman. And yet, in the mind of a man inclined to sensuality, the image of a woman does not always remain pure, but is mixed with a carnal impulse which suggests an action against God's law. Likewise, money and wine are not evil in themselves, but yet they can become a stumbling block due to the impure urges which are added to them. Thus we call «pure» something to which nothing else is added, such as when we speak, for example, of pure gold, pure water, etc. Thus thoughts, too, are pure until something is added to them as an impetus which leads to doing something evil.

3

Where do such impulses to evil come from?

The Fathers compared the human heart to a «promised land», into which the Philistines, the Babylonians and other pagan peoples throw spears and arrows, that is, evil suggestions. These «diabolical», «carnal», «impure» thoughts cannot have their origins in our hearts, since that is created by God. Therefore they come «from outside». They do not belong to our natural way of thinking. And since they remain «outside» us, they are not sins. They constitute an evil only when we consciously and freely welcome them, that is when we identify with them.

4

But in the Gospel it says that evil comes from heart and not from external things (MATT. 15:19). Well?

Yes, but we must be careful about how we explain this passage. Sin comes from the heart of the human person because consent to evil has come from within the person, from their free will. Evil thoughts, passionate desires go round continually, so to speak, around us. Often they fill our fantasy and mind. They constitute human weakness after the sin of the first ancestors. But in themselves they are still not yet true evil. The Church states that concupiscence comes from sin and draws to sin, but in itself it is not sin.

5

So we live in a dangerous state, always exposed to temptation...

Human life on earth is a struggle, says Job (7:1). And a proverb adds that whoever does not want to fight should not even live. But we must not exaggerate the difficulty of this struggle. An ancient mystic author, Pseudo-Macarius, compares our soul to a great city. At the center there is a beautiful castle, close by there is the market square and around there are the suburbs. The enemy, that is original sin, has occupied the suburbs, that is our senses. And it is therefore often there that we feel disturbed. But frequently these disturbances also reach the market place, that is the place where discussions begin to take place about whether we should or shouldn't welcome a thought as ours or whether we must reject it. But in the inner castle, where we are free to be master, sin cannot penetrate unless we open the door by our free consent.

Saint Teresa of Avila, too, speaks of the «inner castle» of our soul, where we can converse with the Lord, the divine Guest, without the outlying disturbances hindering us in any way.

6

Nevertheless, we are internally divided. This is not nice, and perhaps it is even wearing...

Spiritual people try not only to avoid sin, but also to purify the heart, because thus doing the soul can return to inner peace. Monastic authors spoke of ascesis using the Greek term *praxis*, thus indicating spiritual practice. But they distinguish between «external practice» — which one focuses on to avoid sinful acts — and «internal practice» — whose aim is to purify the heart. Often, unfortunately, the moral teaching they propose remains limited to just external practice: «You must not do this, you can do that». And this might explain why very often, when people feel too disturbed, they no longer know what to do and, since the application of the external laws they have does not help them, then, in searching for further solutions, they turn to the most disparate methods proposed by some false mysticism, to doctors, drugs, etc.

It is often forgotten that Christian spirituality offers most effective instructions to acquire peace.

7

Where can these instructions be found?

The monks who chose a life of solitude were particularly expert in achieving inner peace. They sought quiet by fleeing the world. But soon they experienced that solitude alone in itself is not peaceful. Saint Antony the Abbot, for example, went into the desert, but was attacked by «demons», that is by a multitude of thoughts and fantasies which disturbed him. He therefore had to learn how to overcome these «demons». Only after a long inner struggle did he acquire the art of overcoming fantasies. Only then did his solitude become a place of peace. Such an experience was so common, so well-known, that in the Byzantine Empire a state law forbade monks from going out into the desert, in solitude, before having lived the ascetic life in a monastery for ten years. Therefore, before facing the eremitical life, the monks had to have already learned to be masters of their thoughts and fantasies.

8

But are these experiences of the Ancient Monks still accesible and useful to people today?

It is interesting that in our day —precisely because a clear need is felt and requests increase— ancient spiritual texts about the theme of inner struggle are translated and published. To quote a well-known example, suffice to recall how recently the number of translations of Nicodemus of the Holy Mountain's *Philocalia* has increased. The text is a collection of numerous patristic passages in which it is taught how to acquire purity of heart, which is the condition for prayer and tranquility of life.

9

It is said that real sin only happens when there is free consent which unites with the evil thought. But how can we know for sure if whe have freely consented or not?

There are some scrupulous people who in confession accuse themselves of «having had evil thoughts», but do not know how to respond to the question of whether they have consented to them or not. The ancient monks knew that such uncertainty is very harmful to the peace of the soul. Therefore they proposed an accurate analysis of the mental process which occurs on the occasion of inner temptations. Usually five stages of evil penetrating the heart are distinguished: 1) the suggestion, 2) the conversation, 3) the struggle, 4) the consent, 5) the passion.

This obviously needs an explanation.

What is the suggestion?

∽

This first stage is also called «contact». It is the first image provided by the fantasy, the first idea, the first urge. Thus, for example, a miser sees some unguarded money and has an idea: «I could hide it». Likewise, we could have carnal images, thoughts about being better than everyone else, the urge to stop working, etc. In this case we don't decide anything yet, we simply note that the possibility of doing evil offers itself to us, and the evil presents itself in a pleasing manner. The neophytes of the spiritual life are terrified, confess to having had «evil thoughts» even in church and when praying. The story is recounted that Saint Antony the Abbot had led on to the roof one of his disciples who was bitterly complaining about evil thoughts, and he ordered him to catch the wind in his hand. Then, after a while, he said to him: «If you cannot catch the wind, even less can you catch evil thoughts in your hand!» He thus wanted to show that in these first suggestions there is still no guilt and, as long as we live, we will not be able to free ourselves from suggestions. They are like flies that bother us the more we become impatient.

What does «conversation» mean?

∽

This stage recalls the account of *Gen* 3, when Eve enters into conversation with the serpent. If we ignore the suggestion, it goes away just like it had come. But people don't usually do that, they rather let themselves be provoked and start to reflect. So the miser says: «If I take that money, I'll put it in the bank». Then the miser thinks that this is dishonest and, besides, it is also dangerous, since someone might get to know about it. So he thinks it would be best to keep things hidden.

The miser is unable to decide anything, but the question about the money remains in his head all day. The same happens when someone is annoyed with someone. For a long time one thinks about the person who has annoyed you. One thinks about hitting them, offending them, then generously forgiving them, then anew thinking about what could be done to them… It is forgotten only after a long time.

Whose fault are these inner «conversations»? Someone who has decided nothing cannot have sinned. But how much time and vital energy is wasted on these silly inner «dialogues»!

12
Why does the struggle only occupy third place?

We are at the third stage. A thought which, after a long conversation, has wormed its way into the heart, does not let itself be dispelled easily. The sensual person has such a poisonous fantasy of impure images that he/she cannot get rid of them. He/she is still free to not consent. He/she can and must come out of this struggle victorious, but the exertion will be great: he/she must fight. The will must hold firm, he/she must repeat to themselves: «I feel a strong attraction to sin, and yet I do not want to consent, I freely decide the opposite and I am capable of resisting».

13
What is consent?

This is the fourth stage. Whoever has lost the battle decides to carry out, for the first occasion, what the evil thought suggests, gives his/her free consent to the suggestion of evil. In this stage sin in the true and proper sense is committed. And even if it will not be concretized externally, the sin remains internally. It is what morality calls «sin in thought». However, people who are not instructed enough and are not expert confuse the concepts. They believe that the thought of sin is already sinful. Thus such people become scrupulous and confess to not being able to free themselves of «sins in thought». How does one get out of this confusion? One needs to be able to stop and say: «What do I feel, the attraction to sin? Does it please me? Do I feel significantly very attracted to carrying it out? Shall I do it? No! I decide not to do it». This last decision should console us. At the moment we have taken it, we have discovered our freedom. The human person is essentially the one who decides and not the one borne to the attraction of the senses. In such moments, when free consent is given to evil, one also experiences sin.

14
What is passion?

This is the final, most tragic stage. Whoever succumbs to evil thoughts often gradually weakens their character. Thus is born a constant inclination to evil which can grow to the point of being very difficult to resist. It is precisely passion which makes the human person slave to drink, abuse of sex, the explosion of uncontrollable anger, etc. Can one say that in such a person freedom has already been destroyed? There are differing opinions about this. Recently, both some psychologists and, often, some jurists have considered people characterized by strong passions to be abnormal. Therefore they have not accused them of anything but exaggerated weakness. On the contrary, the ancient Fathers, for example like St John Chrysostom, repeated to these type of people, too: «Enough desire!» In the eyes of the Fathers, therefore, the passionate and weak person, too, remains a person, therefore the will is also present in them. But it is as if it had fallen asleep and so needs to be re-awoken. In such a sense, a problem particularly current today is those who take drugs. Experience shows that a special cure is needed to wake and strengthen their will. But extraordinary help from God's grace is needed, too. We remember an ancient monk cured of a strong sexual passion who considered himself, by the grace of Christ, as risen from the dead.

15
So real sin only occurs at the fourth stage?

༄

It is worth repeating: real sin is conditioned by free consent. This should console the scrupulous who are terrified of evil thoughts and desires which they often confess to having had and are so saddened when such thoughts recur even after confession. What must we do, then, when we are assailed by such temptations? We must stop ourselves and say: «What do I want to do? What am I going to decide?» Before God, the human person is the one who freely desires and not the one who feels against his/her own will. The discovery of one's own will is very important for progress in the spiritual life.

But it remains true that evil thoughts which attract our attention are unpleasant. How can one avoid them? To this end spiritual people learned the practice which is called *attention* or *vigilance of the heart*, or *mental sobriety*.

Vigilance of the heart

1

Be vigilant

«Be awake to all the dangers; stay firm in the faith», writes Saint Paul to the Corinthians (*1 Cor* 16:13). A vigilant door-keeper is alert, guards the door so no stranger can enter the house. In a spiritual sense, writes Evagrius, a vigilant guard needs to be put on the door of the heart. This guard never closes his eyes, but examines every thought that presents itself, asking it: «Are you one of ours or from our enemies?»

The five «stages» or «steps» of penetration which described in the previous chapter provide us with a sense of moral security. In fact, we have seen that sin is not committed immediately at the first stage, but only at the fourth, when there is consent. Before that, during the «conversation», we do not sin, nor do we do so during the «struggle». However, it must be said that in these stages we have wasted a lot of time and spiritual energy conversing with the thoughts and weakly resisting their suggestions. Therefore happy is the person who succeeds in defeating the evil thought right from the first suggestion.

2

The example of Jesus

How can the thought which comes on its own, against our will, be banished? From a psychological point of view it is a major problem.

But can a person exist who is free from suggestions? The ascetics asked themselves if Jesus himself was, or if he too was a victim of them. Clearly, for us it is difficult to enter into the inner state of the Savior's soul. However, the gospel does teach us something: Christ, too, was tempted by the devil (*Matt* 4:1-11). And his temptation was similar to our temptations which present themselves in the form of suggestions: «Tell these stones to turn into loaves… Throw yourself down… I will give you all of these if you fall at my feet and worship me». In our human experience —as we have already seen in our description of the process of penetration of the evil thought into the heart— the suggestion is very often followed by the «conversation», that is the dialogue with the thought. In such a conversation the reasons for and against a certain choice are mulled over and weighed up. Jesus avoided such a conversation with suggestion. He simply gave an unhesitating answer to reject what had been suggested to him by Satan. He did as we do when we are concerned and someone suggests to us, for example, to go out with him. Without hesitating we say: «I can't». With our «contradiction» the discourse is closed. This is the only reasonable way to act in such cases. In fact, the briefer and more decisive the answer the more effective it is. Just as how we behave with people who harass us unjustly, so we must act faced with the suggestions of the evil one.

3

Refutng the Devil

The Greek term for this practice of refuting is *antirrhêsis*. It became traditional, because Evagrius wrote a book entitled *Antirrheticus* (*Selection of scripture passages for countering the eight passions*). The author noted that in responding to the devil Jesus used passages from Sacred Scripture: «Man does not live on bread alone, but on every word that comes form the mouth of God… You must not put the Lord your God to the test… You must worship the Lord your God, and serve him alone!» Scripture reveals God's will to us. Its phrases are therefore a weapon against demonic suggestions. In the gospel there are only three sayings quoted against specific suggestions. However, in human life suggestions of evil present themselves in many different forms. But, on the other hand,

Sacred Scripture also contains very many appropriate passages to be proclaimed when an evil thought enters the mind. Evagrius chose the best ones and arranged them according to the eight general categories of evil thoughts: against gluttony, lust, avarice, joylessness, anger, sloth, pride. The monks learned them by heart in order to be ever ready to fight back when temptation appeared. For example, when someone was tempted to concern him/herself uselessly in the affairs of others, he would be advised to say what Jesus said to Saint Peter who wanted to know what would happen to Saint John: «What does it matter to you? You are to follow me» (*John* 21:22).

Often one reads in hagiographic documents that a monk saint «knew the Sacred Scriptures by heart». The modern reader cannot believe it. How, for example, could one remember the lists of the many names contained in the different generations mentioned in the Old Testament? This is a misunderstanding. The expression «to know the whole of Sacred Scripture by memory» points to the art of spiritual direction: when every form of temptation was revealed to the spiritual father who, recognizing the type of temptation, advised on the most appropriate biblical passage to combat it.

4

The power of Jesus' name

The practice of refuting, *antirrhêsis*, therefore seemed to be very useful. And yet to the simple people it occasionally seemed complicated. So the question arose: when temptation arrives, who, at a stroke, can recall an appropriate scripture passage to combat it? Couldn't the practice be somewhat simplified by finding one text suitable for all occasions? Gradually devotees convinced themselves that invoking the name of Jesus «set demons to flight». Therefore the so-called «Jesus Prayer» began to be repeated often. Its formula in the eastern tradition is: «Lord Jesus Christ, Son of God, have mercy on me, a sinner!» Spiritual people commended it as a liberating force for the heart, an easy and effective defense against every temptation and distraction in life.

5

Shouldn't one it be rather the prayer «to Jesus»?

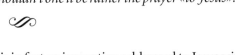

It is in fact an invocation addressed to Jesus with the formula: «Lord Jesus Christ, Son of God, have mercy on me, a sinner!» It is called the «Jesus Prayer» because that is how it was literally translated from the Greek. Eastern monks recite it often, counting the number of invocations on beads similar to those of the Latin rosary. The famous Russian pilgrim tries to attune it by uniting it with the heartbeat and breathing rate. He judges it to be the most effective means of achieving constant prayer. But above all it serves as a «response» to evil thoughts. When, for example, the suggestion arises to get revenge for an offense received, one responds to this thought saying: «Lord Jesus Christ, Son of God, have mercy on me, a sinner». And this is done at the time of any temptation whatsoever.

6

Can one say that in this way evil suggestions are eliminated?

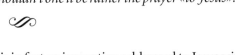

This was presumed by certain quietists. But the Church Fathers said the opposite. The spiritual struggle is the essence of Christian ascesis. If there are moments of respite, these are either a special gift from God or a temptation from the enemy, trying to seduce the person by making him/her wrongly believe they are secure from his snares. John Climacus explained it with this example: sometimes the fox pretends to be asleep, so that the birds come near safely, and then the fox jumps on them all of a sudden; that is what the devil does with souls, too. Therefore in this life evil suggestions are inevitable. There is no time or space so sacred as to be inaccessible to temptation. But the spiritual person, expert in combating temptation, «responds» to it promptly, gains more and more the ability to fight, to the point that in the end they do it even with a certain pleasure, because in doing so they discover their own liberty and supernatural strength.

7

«Spiritual Sobriety», vigilance

Peace of heart is not lasting if it is not protected by constant attention to the disturbances which, coming «from outside», tend to seep into the human person. Therefore, in the language of the ascetics, vigilance of the heart is also called «spiritual sobriety» or simply «watchfulness». The true human act is conscious and free. The more consciousness diminishes, the more one becomes victim of imagination, dreams, obsessive impressions, a type of «lethargy». Even at school, the success of teaching depends on the fact that children «are attentive».

Prayer, raising the mind to God, is unthinkable without attention. Greek authors use a play on words which cannot be translated. Attention in Greek is *prosochê*, prayer is *proseuchê*, two similar words. Therefore they say that the former is mother of the latter. In Byzantine Liturgy, before an important moment the deacon sings precisely this admonition: «*Prosochê*, pay attention!»

8

Is it possible to be always attentive? Who can avoid distractions?

It is difficult to say what comprises attention. A simple definition is «psychological presence to what one is doing». When driving a car and thinking of nothing other than what you see on the road, you are driving in a safe manner. But, on the contrary, you might be thinking about a serious family concern, so that, even though your eyes are still following the road, your «head», your thoughts are elsewhere. At such times an accident can easily happen.

Sometimes even the saints who pray intensely are blind and deaf to what is happening around them. About Saint Bernard one reads that he was unable to say anything about what the ceiling in the cell where he lived was like. Obviously he had something else to think about.

The ability to fully concentrate is an enormous help to work. It is a gift of nature and of God. But not everyone has it. On the contrary, often we meet people incapable of concentrating. They open a book and think about a thousand other things, apart from what they are reading. When they are speaking, they jump from one subject to another. For such people who knows how many and what strange things come into mind when they begin to pray!

9
How do you teach yourself to be attentive?

There are people who suffer from distractions in an abnormal manner. Leaving aside the fact that there are wise doctors who understand how they can be cured, one can note nevertheless that often the lack of concentration is the result of bad habits. In such cases, a strong will can lead to an even rapid improvement. A psychologist had in his room a big fish tank containing various species of rare fish. Next to it there were some seats where he sat his patients who had come to him because they were incapable of paying attention to reading. He then asked each of them to follow with their eyes the movements of just one little fish. At the start they were unable to do so, but after some practice they were able to do it without taking their eyes off the fish even for as long as half an hour. After such exercises, the patients confessed to being able to follow, without being distracted, their own course of mental reading even for half an hour.

But there are times when paying attention is no good whatsoever in being able to do the exercises. For example, a soccer fan follows the match for a long time, without being distracted, even if distracting him would not be easy since it is particularly difficult to distract someone by deflecting attention that has already been focused elsewhere. Correctly, psychologists say that attention is the daughter of interest.

Christian ascetics said the same thing and, applying the principle to prayer, said: concentration on God depends on love, which, according to the ancient monastic saying, is the «ardent fire in the heart which, from the mind lifted up to the Lord, disperses the clouds of evil and useless thoughts».

That leads us to examine the issue of so-called *apatheia*, insensitivity to evil.

10

The eastern Christian idea of apatheia

The term apatheia is of Stoic origin, and so today one still hears the phrase «stoic calmness». In Horace's *Odes* one reads: «Keep a calm mind both in times of difficulties and happiness!» According to the Stoics, this peace of soul is the greatest human happiness. How is it achieved? Christians teach that evil thoughts must be combated. The Stoics had in mind in particular the last stage of the penetration into the heart, that of the passion. Passion in Greek is *pathos*. Denial is expressed through use of the prefix «a»; so, putting the two together leads to the term *apatheia*, indicating the state of the person who has eliminated the passions, and is «beyond every fear, sadness, concupiscence and voluptuousness» (Epictetus).

Four fundamental passions

Passion is a perceptible movement of attraction or repulsion toward something. So, for example, one says someone is a «passionate card player», or that a nationalist feels a «passionate aversion» toward the representative of another people, or that a person plays the violin «with passion», or again «a young boy loves a girl with a strong passion». From these few examples we see that many types of passion exist. All of them disturb serenity and diminish our freedom. Epictetus proposed once again the scheme the Stoics had identified to indicate «four fundamental passions». Our tranquility, the Stoics said, can be disturbed both by something evil and by something joyful, that is both by the evil and the good that arouses us. If evil is present, we are sad; if we foresee it for the future, we are fearful. When we enjoy good things in the present time, we provoke intense delight, when we think that we can enjoy it in the future, concupiscence arises within us. There are, therefore, four chief passions: distress, fear, voluptuousness and concupiscence. They can be compared to four argumentative women in the same house. There will be no peace until all four are banished.

12

Can all the passions be eliminated? And moreover: would it be useful to become completely insensitive?

When eastern Christians adopted the term *apatheia* to express the ideal of inner peace, they were sharply criticized by Saint Jerome. He rebuked authors for wanting to make the human person an angel or a stone devoid of feelings. But angels, like God, cannot have perceptible movements, because these are linked to the body. On the contrary, the human person cannot live without perceiving the attraction of the senses, otherwise he/she would either be like an insensitive stone or be ill. Isn't it perhaps natural to feel hunger, thirst, the attraction of playing, love? Therefore, scholastic authors also rejected *apatheia*. However, there is a need to distinguish between the good passions, that is the attraction to good, from the evil passions which drive us toward evil. As regards the good passions, the only thing that is asked is that they be under one's own control. In this sense, even anger can be good, when for example in just measure one rages against evil, as Jesus did in chasing the vendors from the Temple (*Matt* 21:22ff.).

To avoid misunderstanding, there is a need first to better define what is meant by the term «passion». For the eastern authors it indicates the inclination to evil. Considered in this way, it is therefore desirable that such «passions» be destroyed and the heart be completely pure of them.

On the contrary, western authors use the term passion for every perceptible attraction both to evil and good. They therefore distinguish the «ordered» passions from the «disordered». Consequently, perfection consists not in eradicating or destroying the passions, but only in controlling them, in «ordering them». The passions are therefore like horses with bridles: they have to be led along the correct path, but not weakened or killed.

13

So, how should the apatheia *so praised by the Greek Fathers be understood?*

It is not the absence of suffering or sensitivity. «Fakirism» in itself is not a human perfection. The delicacy of natural feelings is a positive value. One cannot pretend that the perfect human being is free from the «suggestions» of evil thoughts. They come to that person, too. But —Evagrius says— «they no longer shake that person», they are no longer dangerous for him/her. Could one say that such a person is already fault-less? That would be saying too much. Adam sinned even in paradise. The choice of good or evil remains always free. But for the person who has reached *apatheia*, the choice of good is easy and joyful. It corresponds to the strength of the pure soul. Strong youngsters rejoice when they can fight against the weakest, and when they are attacked they laugh. Faced with evil thoughts that come into the mind, the free person experiences a similar joy. He/she laughs at such thoughts and has no fear of coming away from them perturbed. Commenting on this inner strength, Saint John Climacus calls *apatheia* «resurrection of the soul prior to that of the body».

14

Apatheia *and charity*

Far from being a sort of deathlike insensitivity, *apatheia*, Christian indifference is rather a «consuming fire», the divine fire in the heart which burns all temptations as soon as they appear. The example provided by Saint Ephraim is of a very popular kind, but nonetheless very expressive. He says: when the soup is hot, no fly can get to it, the insects go there only when it has cooled down; likewise the heart which burns for love of God destroys the thoughts which oppose it. «If we truly love God, our very charity itself banishes evil passions», says Saint Maximus the Confessor. It is charity which brings together all the forces of the human person under the direction of the Holy Spirit.

According to Vladimir Losskij, this is the ideal incarnated in the Virgin Mary, who «represents the summit of holiness… she was without sin under the universal dominion of sin»; «sin was unable to come to fruition in her person».

The discernment of spirits

1

Dismiss thoughts? Certainly not all of them!

Up to now we have spoken about evil thoughts that are the cause of sin. But if it is true that every evil action begins with a thought, it is equally true that good, too, has its origins in thought, a good thought called «inspiration». Therefore there is a need to know how to distinguish between these two types of thoughts. The biographies of the saints recount how many experiences they had in this field and also how many mistakes they made not knowing «how to distinguish the spirits».

2

Why talk about «spirits» if we are dealing with thoughts?

Chapter 12 of the *Book of Revelation* picks up again and completes the *Genesis* account about the origin of sin, summarizing in a few words the Bible doctrine about the devil and his role in salvation history, and portraying the personal clash which sets Christ against the «seducer», «the prince of this world». In this perspective, the Fathers interpret different events in the life of Christ. The spiritual life of Christians, too, is seen as a battle against the demons. The Bible presents to the human person choices that he/she cannot avoid. However, sometimes these choices are thwarted. In fact, in opposition to the divine voice, to the voice of conscience, another voice makes itself heard: that of Satan's suggestions for evil. How can one be discerned from the other? In the New Testament epistles the explicit expression is used «distinguishing spirits» (*1 Cor* 12:10; cf. *1 John* 4:1). «Discernment of thoughts» indicates the area where the spiritual battle begins and where fundamentally things are already decided.

3

Who is capable of distinguishing good from evil thoughts?

✍

Witnessing to the voice of God was the task of the prophets, and the Wisdom books were written to teach to distinguish the voice of wisdom from that of foolishness. This problem did not cease to occupy a major place in spiritual literature. But the art of discerning thoughts is in the first place a gift of God. For Saint John the spiritual experience is an «anointing», a state of light (*1 John* 2:20, 27). Saint Antony the Abbot said: «Much prayer and ascesis is needed so that, having received from the Spirit the charism of discernment of the spirits, one can know what concerns each demon…». Furthermore, this knowledge is the fruit of lengthy observation. Through experience, in fact, one can acquire a special «sense», a spiritual intuition, up to the point of becoming capable of recognizing where every thought would lead us.

4

Today are there still prophets capable of interpreting the voice of God?

✍

The question is entirely justified. In the Old Testament one reads of prophets, and also in the New there is reference to their presence in the Christian communities. The gift of prophecy was particularly appreciated by the Church Fathers. Why, then, does it seem that today they no longer exist? The word «prophet» received a pejorative significance due to the spread of false prophets emerging from the Montanist sect. But if «prophet» means someone who speaks in God's name, such a charism remains essential for the Church. It is interesting to note that in the Eastern Churches a good spiritual father was called a prophet. His main function was in fact to recognize and state what inspiration is good and which instead must be considered as a suggestion of evil. Therefore people were advised, especially the young, to reveal «every thought» to the spiritual father and therefore leave him to decide what had to be done.

5
But whoever has a suspect thought is not going to voluntarily reveal it to someone else!

In fact Saint Ignatius expresses this experience with an example. A false lover —he says— when he wants to seduce a young girl, always wants to remain hidden and wants everything to be kept secret. Because, if the girl reveals it to his father, he would know how the story is going to end. Likewise, the devil, too, when he suggests some deceit, tries to convince us not to talk about it to the spiritual father. In fact, when an evil thought is revealed, it is easily overcome. For this reason there is insistence on the need to have a good spiritual father, that is to have someone to whom one can reveal one's own thoughts in complete trust, above all at the start of the journey in the spiritual life, when for a beginner discernment is still extremely difficult.

6
But how is it possible to reveal every thought to the spiritual Father?

One must avoid falling into misunderstandings. When we speak of «thought», we don't mean here everything we think, but just the suggestions, that is the inspirations which bring us to deciding to do or not do a certain thing, starting from the recognition of its presumed or real goodness. Therefore it is prudent to take counsel, not from the first person who comes, but to turn to a «spiritual father», that is someone of whom we have no doubt that he has the help of the Holy Spirit and knowledge of the human heart. Only the person who has these requisites can tell, like a prophet, what God desires of us.

7
Is it just a few people who are like this?

୧/୨

It is true that you don't bump into them all the time, but there is a need to look for them carefully. On the other hand, already the ancient monks complained about not succeeding in finding a good spiritual father. There was then the idea of establishing certain principles, certain rules, by which to recognize goodness or evil from the inner suggestions. An interesting example of this attempt is found in the *Spiritual Exercises* of Saint Ignatius of Loyola. He felt a great need for the ability to distinguish between the two types of suggestions, because after his conversion he had made mistakes again, considering to be divine inspiration what was just an illusion. Subsequently, led by his own experience, he established for himself and others some «rules for the discernment of spirits». But already before him many other spiritual figures had had the same experience. Therefore, some «rules» had become traditional.

8
What is the fundamental rule?

୧/୨

When Saint Antony the Abbot retreated into the desert, he had his first experience of discernment of thoughts. They can be distinguished according to the effect they produce. Good suggestions lead to an «inexpressible joy, cheerfulness, courage, inner renewal, steadfastness of thought, strength and love for God»; the others, instead, bring with them «fear in the soul, disturbance and confusion of thought, dejection, hatred against the ascetics, sloth, grief, remembrance of kinsfolk, fear of death and finally evil desires, disregard of virtue and unsettled habits». This rule was simplified in the saying: «What disturbs comes from the devil, while God gives peace to the heart».

9
Can this rule aleays be applied?

Basically it is always valid, however its application cannot be automatic. In fact, when one is almost softened in one's evil habits, then to be shaken and, in a certain sense, disturbed is the work of divine grace. Therefore there is a need to distinguish even the different feelings of peace. Peace does not always come from God, there is also an illusory peace which comes from the world. But only the gospel promises us true peace, which is lasting and leads to good.

10
In fact we often feel disturbed. Is this normal?

First experiences are not easily discernible. Usually we become aware of our inner state only when, in a certain sense, it is more lasting. So we say to others: «Leave me in peace, I'm in a bad mood, and it's not going away!» Spiritual books do not speak of bad moods, but use the word «desolation». They note how it influences our relations with God and the fulfillment of religious duties. In the *Exercises* Saint Ignatius describes it in this way: «I call desolation… the darkness of the soul, turmoil of the mind, inclination to low and earthly things, restlessness resulting from many disturbances and temptations which lead to loss of faith, loss of hope, and loss of love. It is also desolation when a soul finds itself completely apathetic, tepid, sad, and separated, as it were, from its Creator and Lord». In modern terminology one can translate this by speaking about revulsion, frustration, and doubts about everyone and everything.

11

How should one behave in such a state of inner desolation?

Everyone says: «You have to react, the human person must not let themselves be driven by their disturbance». But how and where do you start? The first step is to gain trust in one's own freedom. A bad frame of mind suggests to us a multitude of false projects. And it is logical. It is like when scales are broken: they don't weigh properly. For this reason, we must be steadfast and not change decisions already taken, when we felt well. Doing this is a wonderful experience: we discover that we are strong and capable of doing the opposite of what the current bad frame of mind is suggesting we do.

12

But loathing is debilitating; it removes the will to resist!

And yet at such moments we must re-awaken precisely this will to resist, to do the opposite of what we will be naturally inclined to undertake. Saint Ignatius suggests an example which might seem banal, but expresses the idea well. He says that the devil behaves toward us like an argumentative woman. When there is strong resistance to her, she shuts up. On the other hand, when one loses heart and begins to flee, she pursues with more ferocity.

13
Why experience such unpleasant moods?

ॐ

To face these circumstances spiritual writers recall the biblical story of Job. All his suffering became a test of his virtue. Spiritual desolation is therefore a hard test, especially for those who wish to devote themselves to a life of prayer. An example has been given by Saint Teresa of Avila, a contemplative nun, who suffered desolation for some years, but subsequently was rewarded with great visions. Nevertheless every Christian needs to be in some way tested by desolation. Only thus in fact is one made aware that true devotion cannot be measured just by the intensity of the good feelings experienced. Everything does not go well just when we feel well.

14
But the tests must not be exaggerated!

ॐ

In fact God never tests human beings beyond the just limits and always gives a special strength to overcome external and internal difficulties. In addition, in desolation we must always have the hope that the current difficult moment is a state which will pass.

In spiritual evolution a certain rule has even been identified. When one decides to set out on the path of spiritual life, at the start, usually, one feels encouraged and full of enthusiasm. Then comes a state of dryness of the soul, of loathing for things spiritual, but subsequently there comes a consolation more solid and lasting than the previous one.

15

Everyone has their personal weaknesses. Many people excuse themselves saying: «this is my character». But can one's own defects be overcome?

Just as there are bodily sicknesses, so there are also weaknesses of the soul. One person tends to be glum, another get annoyed easily, another is lazy by nature. At this juncture, too, we can recall an example from Saint Ignatius. He says that the devil behaves like a military leader who wants to take over a castle. He first analyzes the weak points in order to attack beginning precisely with them. Just like a good defender who puts his best soldiers in the guard posts anticipating they may be attacked, so we must do, too: focus attention where we err most easily and are most vulnerable. Therefore we must know ourselves well to protect ourselves well.

16

But how can one know oneself?

Experience teaches everyone. In this regard the exercise known as an «examination of conscience», which is recommended to be done especially in the evening, before going to sleep, is important. But it is mistaken to think that in the examination attention should be focused just on sins. It is even more important to ask oneself these questions: «Today which thoughts have weighed on my heart and occupied my mind? What do they produce in my mind? Do they disturb or bring peace? Where do they want to lead me?» Thoughts are like friends. Soon one learns to distinguish among them the true from the false. So the saints said they could already recognize good suggestions from evil ones by their «smell», by the way in which they presented themselves.

17

Saints have often described their experiences for the Disciples. Where can one read them?

Many spiritual authors have written about «discernment of the spirits».

Already in the 5th century Diadochus of Photice collected what the Fathers said about the matter. We have already quoted Saint Ignatius of Loyola who, having had experience practically alone, wrote about what he had experienced, setting out some rules of conduct for the discernment of spirits.

Lorenzo Scupoli, too, expressed the principles of discernment in a book entitled *The Spiritual Combat*. But what became more famous was Evagrius' catalog (end of the 4th century) on the «eight evil spirits», which has a list, aiming to be complete, of the various types of temptation which definitely lead to evil.

The eight evil thoughts

1

Is it possible to draw up a catalog of all the evil thoughts?

At first sight it seems impossible. In fact the suggestions of evil are so numerous and diverse that no one can succeed in listing them completely. But it must also be said that certain vices are frequent. Therefore literature from the Hellenist era already offers lists of vices. On the other hand, from the start of the New Testament we find different examples of them. So it was at the end of the 4th century that Evagrius proposed the list of eight «generic thoughts» which then became traditional, because in them can be categorized and described the various temptations which usually attack a person.

2

So what is thid traditional catalog?

In his *Praktikos* Evagrius expresses it this way: «There are eight generic thoughts, that contain within themselves every [tempting] thought: first is that of gluttony; and with it, sexual immorality; third, love of money; fourth, sadness; fifth, anger; sixth, sloth; seventh, vainglory; eighth, pride».

3

But it's the same as the list of the «seven capital vices, the seven deadly sins…»

Yes, it is the same. However, Saint Gregory the Great changed the order. Pride was put first as the root of all vices. In addition, vainglory and pride were considered to be one vice and so the number was reduced to seven. The Greek term «acedia» was not well understood, therefore one spoke simply of «laziness». The completely perverse sadness which manifests itself when we feel sad, not happy, at the success of our neighbor, became defined as «envy», a term which in the Latin catalog replaced «sadness». Thus we arrive at the list presented in our catechisms. It matters little if the list is proposed in this or another order. What is important is that spiritual authors try to analyze what these vices consist of, what thoughts suggest them to us and what remedies can be used to combat them.

4
What is gluttony?

There is a popular saying: «Eat to live, don't live to eat». The reason for eating is therefore the health of the body. But the body must be kept in such a state to be able to serve the soul. Bodily needs are different depending on one's own constitution, the work being done, the circumstances in which the food is taken on. Nature itself, in animals and plants, points out to us how we must behave. In fact, plants and animals search and take from nature what they need, nothing more and nothing less. Saint Basil shows the validity of this natural law with many concrete examples. The human person must therefore follow it consciously, freely, with the aim desired by God. The evil thought of gluttony, writes Cassian, suggests to us eating before the set time, encourages us to eat too much and makes us look for food not according to its real benefit, but simply to satisfy gluttony. It is said that at table the educated human being gives the impression of being able, at any moment, to be called elsewhere and being able to get up gladly. For the Christian we can also suggest that what characterizes him/her is the fact of being always ready to give precedence, in the face of sensitive pleasures, to the spirit.

5
Fornication

To Buddha is attributed the saying: «The stimulus of sexual instinct is sharper than the needle used to put wild elephants to sleep, it burns stronger than fire and possesses an arrow which penetrates right into the soul». The intensity of such an instinct is not astounding, since it is the preservation instinct of the human race. However, it must be stated that humans must preserve themselves and multiply in a human manner, by free and moral decisions. The applications of sexual continence are, in practical life, most numerous. Books on morality are full of them.

The first and most important support in preserving chastity is to learn to distinguish well. To the consolation of those who feel tormented and invaded by doubts, the Church never tires of repeating what has been laid down: «Concupiscence comes from sin and pushes toward sin, but it is not sin». Not feeling any temptation against chastity is an exceptional gift from God. When suggestions come to us pushing us toward immoral acts, when fantasy presents us with impure images, we must learn to stop and say to ourselves: «What do I want and decide? The opposite of the suggestion!» There are also means which recommend themselves to help pre-empt an excess of sexual feelings: custody of the senses, prayer, but especially constant work. If idleness is the father of vices, work can make you forget them and calm the soul.

6
Avarice

Frugality is a virtue. It is not easy, however, to tell when it is transformed into avarice. Four rules alert and warn the person who saves too much.

It is forbidden to appropriate things against the law, against the Decalogue, by means of theft.

Goods can be acquired honestly. The miser thinks that all he/she has acquired is his/hers in an absolute way and there is no obligation to give anything to anyone, not even what is superfluous.

The diligent person looks to see where they can earn money. The miser does it in such a way that, apart from earning money, he/she loses interest in other values. He/she only seeks those activities from which there is financial gain.

Not just religious but also lay people must practice in a certain way the virtue of poverty, that is they must seek the welfare which is appropriate to their state, without exaggeration. Misers place too much trust in their money, forget God, are hard toward their neighbor and thus, in the end, their own lives suffer. Apart from money they have no interests, neither cultural nor any others linked to healthy relaxation. They guard their treasure on earth and not in heaven (cf. *Matt* 6:19ff.).

7
Sadness, Envy

When we are sad, we express the conviction that something is not as it should be, that we want something that is not there. It is therefore a type of loathing. But the Christian must loathe sin as the one real evil. If, on the contrary, sadness about life as it is, the company of others, the fact that we are alone, etc., assails us, then there is always some deficiency in faith in God's Providence and his work. Sadness is dangerous. It paralyzes the courage to carry on in work and prayer and makes us disagreeable to our neighbors. The monastic writers, who devote long descriptions to this vice, call it the spiritual life's worst enemy.

There are different types of sadness. One of them is dissolute from the outset: the sadness at the good enjoyed by someone else. This type of sadness can also be defined as envy. According to Saint John Chrysostom, the envious person is worse than the miser. In fact, if the latter is happy with what he has, the envious person toils so that others have nothing: «Perhaps he himself does not get up because he is lazy, but he is capable of jumping out of bed to make the other person, who is on his feet, fall». If it is true that there are often subtle feelings of displeasure when another person succeeds, there is a need to be vigilant and dedicate oneself with a degree of goodwill to not give into them.

8

Is it acceptable to try to outdo someone else's success?

ↄ⁊ↄ

It cannot be denied that life in current society is a continuous struggle to boost one's own occupational, economic, sporting success, etc. What is important is that it should all be done honestly, without grievances of antipathy toward others. Then when it is a matter of competing for a greater possession of spiritual goods, this type of emulation is recommendable. So we read of Saint Antony the Abbot who retreated in the face of everyone else in everything, only wishing to overcome everyone in virtue. But it must be the truly authentic virtues, so that competition does not boil over.

9

Anger

ↄ⁊ↄ

Anger begins with feelings of antipathy against what presents itself —really or just in the imagination— as an obstacle in our path. So suddenly we want to put it aside. We get an idea about how to do this. Thus anger is born, which can be just or unjust.

What anger can be considered just? The only real obstacle to good is evil. Therefore, we can and must kindle in ourselves anger against evil. But it must be a real evil and not imaginary. In the full sense of the word we must therefore get angry about sin, the devil, about evil thoughts. As regards people, anger is just only if it leads to good, to the defeat of evil and so to the benefit, not the harm, of one's neighbor. The image of a just anger is, as we have already recalled, Christ who banishes the vendors from the Temple (*Mark* 11:15ff; *John* 2:14ff.). It is understood that anger must be proportionate, controlled, and moderate.

10

Uncontrolled anger

What anger is to be considered unjust? From the feeling of displeasure there often stems hatred and a desire for revenge. We experience pleasure at someone else's disgrace, we humiliate that person by words and malign them in front of others. Then we move to action. More often anger manifests itself in an explosion of feelings which are stronger than sane judgment. Such an angry person is, according to Saint John Climacus, a mad person, a «voluntary epileptic». One cannot speak with such a person until the anger impulse has ceased. The best advice to give him/her is that of some popular phrases: «Breathe deeply», «Count to ten», «Chop wood, but not on somebody else's head».

Much more dangerous is the anger which remains in the soul even when the explosion of feelings has already passed. So one begins to reflect coldly on revenge, one refuses to forgive. According to Saint Gregory of Nyssa, a person who behaves in this way cuts themselves off from the kingdom of God. They themselves won't be pardoned, because they do not pardon others; God will not intervene on their behalf, because they want to want to bring about justice on their own.

11

How is the explosion of anger overcome?

It is recounted in the *Lives* of the Desert Fathers that a short-tempered man was healed in this way. He was made to repeat this sort of prayer: «We give thanks to you, Lord, that we have no need of you, because we will get justice on our own». Saint Dorotheus compares the angry person to a dog which bites a stone and, in its blindness, doesn't see the person who has thrown the stone. Therefore one has to attempt to reason.

«Even if you are angry, you must not sin!» we read in Saint Paul (*Eph* 4:26). The apostle of the nations had an explosive temperament. He knew from experience how one can get angry when suddenly evil, dishonesty and problems specifically combine. But this impulse must not lead us to sin, so as not to get rid of one evil with another. Moreover, Saint Paul stipulates a prudent time to calm down, up to sunset: «Never let the sun set on your anger» (*Eph* 4:26). Anger is definitively healed by means of the opposite virtues: meekness, patience, faith in providence.

12

Sloth

The Greek term *akêdia* has a broader meaning than the corresponding Latin term «laziness». It means a general state of loathing, tiredness, disinterest, «lukewarmness». It is also called the «midday demon» (cf. *Ps* 90:6), the one which assails the monk in the middle of the day, when, that is, the passion, the desire to work passes. Monks, in fact, got up very early in the morning and therefore in the middle of the day fatigue crept in. In an allegorical way, the same is true for the «midday of life», when youthful enthusiasm fades. Evagrius was convinced that this is a «most dangerous demon», because the disgusted and the lazy person have no will to resist, and therefore the enemy finds in them an easy prey.

13
Spiritual idleness

∽

This is what the Latin authors call sloth. Ludovico Da Ponte lists nine manifestations of it: 1) an exaggerated fear of the obstacles one might meet; 2) an aversion to everything that might be tiring; 3) negligence in observing the commandments, order, the rules; 4) instability in the good, in keeping intentions; 5) inability to resist temptation; 6) antipathy to those who are zealous and who become obnoxious because of their diligence and observance of the rules; 7) wasting valuable time; 8) the freedom which is granted to the senses, to curiosity, to the pleasure of self-enjoyment and using everything; 9) negligence in the principle duties of one's state, forgetting one's ultimate end, ignoring religious reasons for action.

14
Tepidness according to Saint Bernard

∽

For Saint Bernard, «tepidness» is the «shadow of death»; the tepid person is a like an uncultivated vine, a house without doors and windows. Tepidness deprives the person of spiritual joy. The effort of the day increases and, at the same time, its merits decrease. It is like a worm which at the roots devours the principle virtues from within, even if outside everything continues as normal. The lazy person hides his talents in the ground (*Matt* 25:25ff). He has no desire to be either too good or too evil. Therefore these words apply to him: «I know all about you: how you are neither cold nor hot. I wish you were one or the other, but since you are neither, but only lukewarm, I will spit you out of my mouth» (*Rev* 3:15-16).

15

Pride

Everyone agrees that pride could be defined as the summit of all the vices and sins. On the other hand, even good people confess to having «thoughts of pride» which cannot be so wicked. So we distinguish, even without really being aware of it, two types of pride: serious and less serious. Eastern authors write of two similar vices, and yet so different: vanity and pride.

In both cases, we claim some good and, for this, we want to be respected: but that good is not our credit. We seek the glory. But this glory can serious or «vain»: so we can boast about something which is worthy of admiration or love to be praised for small, ridiculous, vain things.

In the eyes of the ascetics, the only thing which merits glory is grace, participation in God's life. It is only the Lord who makes us participants in his glory, and so the Christian does not claim it for him/herself. He/she firmly believes that it is an undeserved gift from God. The classic image of pride is therefore the Pharisee who prays: «I thank you, God, that I am not grasping, unjust, adulterous like the rest of mankind, and particularly that I am not like this tax collector here» (*Luke* 18:11). The pride person needs admiration and veneration for what, without credit, he/she has received from God and, for this, they think themselves better than others.

16

Pride —«the last demon»

Rightly it is pointed that it is precisely those who strive to lead a spiritual life who are largely exposed to the danger of real pride. Such a vice is the «last demon» which attacks those who have freed themselves from the «preceding seven». And it is stronger than all the others. It arouses in conscience a feeling of superiority over one's neighbor because of one's own good works, theological awareness, and vocation to the religious state.

It is said that pride comes before a fall. The proud person falls easily into sin. The theologian proud of his knowledge in the end professes his errors. «The self-sufficiency of one's own judgment is», according to Theodoret of Cyrus, the most serious illness of intellectuals who have lost any humility. «They disapprove of any initiative and the advice of others. Their preferred saying is: You do it as I want, or I refuse to collaborate».

17

Conceit

Vanity is a much lesser vice. There are those who allow themselves to be admired for their luxuriant hair, or their beautiful voice, or their intellectual ability, or their noble origins; those who seek glory in «futile» things, which count for little when compared to the real values of life. Saint Francis de Sales says that, even though it is a ridiculous «real passion» (despite that, people succeed in boasting about it!), it has a tough life: it dies, it is said «only half an hour after the death of the person». Right up to the last breath we are tied by human respect. In its most developed state, vanity leads to a lack of sincerity, lies, disputes arise, money is squandered. Also here one speaks of «human respect», but in the worst sense of the term: in order not to lose admiration, people commit vices and, in order to be praised by sinners, also commit sins.

The spiritual authors compare conceit to a thief who accompanies a traveler pretending to be headed for the same place, but who then, unexpectedly, robs him. The vain person often works, keeps the commandments, goes to church. The more zealous they are, the more they desire to be praised.

But in the end, they lose the credit acquired through their good works because, in fact, they have not been undertaken for God, but for vainglory. So what often happens is what Saint Paul wrote: that «it was to shame the wise that God chose what is foolish by human reckoning, and to shame what is strong that he chose what is weak by human reckoning; those whom the world thinks common and contemptible are the ones that God has chosen —those who are nothing at all to show up those who are everything. The human race has nothing to boast about to God» (*1 Cor* 1:27-29).

18
Can one say that pride is the root of all other vices?

Saint Gregory the Great states this. So in his catalog he puts it first. For Evagrius the root of all eight vices is love of self (in Greek *philautia*), others call it «self-will».

19
But is it really evil to love oneself?

Here one needs to be careful not to fall into misunderstanding. The gospel tells us to love one's neighbor as oneself (cf. *Matt* 22:39), it does not say on the other hand to «not love oneself». Scholastics repeated the maxim: «Whoever is not good toward himself, will not be good even to others». Christianity wants to unite both loves, of self and others, in one love. Whoever rejects this union possesses self-love, but on its own it is self-centered, perverse. Loving self, the egoist also destroys himself, because he breaks the relationships with others and thereby diminishes his being «person». Saint Maximus the Confessor defined *philautia*: «love of self against self». True love is the source of all virtues, selfishness is the root of all vices.

20

But how does one not have one's own will?

Using this term, too, there is a need to be careful not create misunderstanding. Free will is one of the greatest gifts from God. «To save oneself», writes Saint John Chrysotom, «it is enough to desire». To weaken the will means making the human person less capable of both human work and the spiritual perfection to which the person aspires. In this context, the exhortations of Saint Dorotheus of Gaza, of Saint Benedict and others who strictly advised to «completely destroy one's own will» in order to be able to accept God's will or the will of the legitimate superior therefore seem strange.

We have already said that the origin of every evil is an evil thought, a suggestion of sin. To that is added an attraction for the forbidden object: the tendency to avarice, for the desire to drink, etc. We know that we can and must resist these suggestions. But sometimes we get the desire to accept them in a way which seems acceptable. So, for example, one tries to justify avarice by the need to save, one calls refusal to forgive a «sense for justice», etc. Various authors call «one's own will» this tendency to justify with holy pretexts the inclination toward evil. Taken in this sense, it goes without saying that it must be destroyed before it becomes the origin of all the problems. The corrupt person does not just commit crimes, but succeeds in justifying them to everyone. It is a sad situation, and it is even more so when it is apparently devout people who love to justify their own hypocrisy even by using passages from Sacred Scripture. The only remedy for this perversion is to sincerely seek the will of God and submit oneself to the one whom transmits it spiritually.

Personal experience

1

Temptations that appear to be good

∽

The catalog of the eight evil thoughts (or the seven capital vices) is like the foundation of Christian morality manuals which attempt to list all the cases which constitute sin in an «objective» way, valid for everyone. The thoughts which suggest such action are certainly immoral. But not all thoughts that enter into our minds are so clearly specific. Authors who are expert in the spiritual life observe that the devil sometimes takes the form of the angel of light (cf. 2 *Cor* 11:14) and deceives under the appearance of good. So, for example, a suggestion at the outset seems good, but only subsequently, through one's own experience, is it perceived that it has led us to evil. To Saint Ignatius, shortly after his conversion, it seemed a godly proposal to do a radical fast. But it resulted in a serious stomach illness. Ignatius subsequently recognized that he had allowed himself to be deceived, not recognizing the trickery hidden under the false appearance of good. That happened because his soul, as he himself confesses, was still unversed in the art of spiritual combat.

2

Is it not too late when we become aware of having had this sad experience?

∽

Of course, and it is precisely for that reason it is recommended that suggestions that are perceived internally be tackled with the advice of a spiritual father. Experts in the spiritual life acquire a sharper sense and succeed in distinguishing the angelic thought from the devilish thought by its «smell». It is the same for people. A person says to me: «At the start I don't pay attention to what someone is saying to me, but instead I listen to their voice. In this way, I am rarely deceived by beautiful words. By the voice itself I pick up if there is some deceit there». It is interesting to note that such observations can also be made about the thoughts that come to us. Saint Ignatius speaks about rules «for greater discernment of spirits» suitable for those who have already made some progress in the inner life. In these cases one is less attentive to what the thought is suggesting, but more attentive to the way in which the thought presents itself to the soul. In this way Saint Antony the Abbot, too, learned to distinguish the spirits: noting the different psychological states that the thoughts produce in the soul.

3

We have already noted the fundamental rule: what disturbs comes from the devil…

But we have also noticed that the principle cannot be applied automatically. Furthermore, the disturbance which one experiences can be very subtle, not easily perceptible… Saint Ignatius states: «To those who progress from good to better, the good angel sweetly and gently touches the soul, like a drop of water penetrating a sponge. But the action of the evil spirit upon such souls is violent, noisy and disturbing. It may be compared to a drop of water falling upon a stone».

4

But what if this distrubance is not noticed immediately?

The development of the thought must be followed. Ignatius describes it thus: «We must pay great attention to the course of thoughts; if the beginning, the middle and the end are all good and tend solely toward the good, it is a sign of the good angel. But if the course of the thought ends in something bad, of a distracting tendency, or less good than what the soul had previously proposed to do, or if it weakens or disquiets or disturbs the soul, taking away its peace, tranquility and quiet, which it had before, it is a clear sign that it proceeds from the evil spirit, enemy of our good and eternal salvation».

5

There is a saying wich needs an explanation: thought leads to something evil or futile. How many meaningless things pass our mind! Are they so harmful?

The Russian spiritual author Theophan the Recluse judges these thoughts severely. He really believes they can be more harmful than explicitly evil thoughts. He does not admit that the honest person is too concerned in thinking about sinful plans. How much valuable time is often wasted fantasizing about useless things! It is said of certain people that they live focused to such a degree that they don't notice what they are talking about. Theophan says ironically: «Focused, yes, but on stupidities!» Therefore, if there is not a true and proper tendency to evil there, it is also true that in this way much valuable time is wasted. What is more: this is followed by a sense of emptiness in the heart and a growing despondency which weakens the strength of the soul.

6

Isn't fantasy a natural force which develops according to its own laws?

But yes! One day a doctor sent a patient to a colleague, with a letter in which he had written: «It seems to me that the poor lady is not ill at all, unless in her own fantasy». The recipient replied: «Her illness is very serious, since it is the fantasy, a very important capacity in our lives, that is sick». The already-quoted spiritual author Theophan is of the same opinion, judging it very dangerous to let the images of fantasy run on, without any control in the mind. Internal or external images are like the «raw material» which must be used to build a sound opinion, a judgment. Reason is the constructing architect. If this remains inactive, images, the «raw material», build up in the confusion. An «inner castle» is not built in the mind, but a sort of heap of intellectual ruins. People affected by this illness can be recognized easily: they are unable to speak nor think with any discipline, they jump from one topic to another, since they are incapable of following a coherent line in any discourse.

7

Not just fantasy's images, but also reasoning can be futile!

Certainly. Theophan warns us about this danger, too. Even more than fantasy, reason is a most precious gift from God which must guide us on the path of life. This, its vital function, must not be lost. Theophan tried to distinguish, following the Greek Fathers and idealistic German philosophy, the two terms: «reason» and «intellect». «Reason», he says, works automatically. It distinguishes the true from the false, but is not concerned with the value its judgment has for life. «Intellect», on the other hand, judges the value of the thoughts which occupy the mind.

According to Theophan, «rationalism» is another dangerous epidemic of our time, similar to that provoked by the abuse of fantasy. The «rationalist», in the pejorative sense of the word, wastes a lot of energy posing him/herself problems which reason alone cannot solve or busying him/herself with issues that are not his/her concern. Meanwhile he/she loses sense of what is directly of concern in life. Thus, as regards the religious life, rationalists want to resolve the mysteries of faith, but they do not ask the question about how to live them in order to be saved.

8

How can we know in advance if a problem is important or not for our lives?

Spiritual authors have given us some practical, but wise advice: «*Age quod agis*», be concerned with what you have to do now! Every moment has its need. The time of prayer is not suitable to think about work. But a definite work needs all the attention to be focused on its being executed properly and not focused on what has to be done later. When we speak with someone, it is good to concentrate on what is being said, but this is best forgotten when we go to sleep. In the recollections of a spiritual father one reads that a young monk asked him why he was unable to live with tranquility in the monastery. The spiritual father said to him: «You will never be calm, you will never find peace. When it is winter you think impatiently about when spring will arrive. At Easter you are thinking about work in the fields in summertime. When you are working you are concerned and think about when work will be over and, when the time to rest has come, you are terrified by how much work you have to do. The fact is your head is never with you, it runs on ahead and you never manage to catch up with it».

9

From this does it follow that thoughts that are not consistent with life must be considered harmful?

In fact, this is an important principle in discernment of the spirits. It can be explained with an analogy taken from the world of art. A professor from the Academy of Fine Arts was giving his marks to work done by the students. One of the pictures was judged to be awful. In the eyes of an untrained person who was present at the marking, the professor's judgment seemed to be unjust, he liked the picture that was considered so negatively, a delicately-drawn picture of a young girl with a bunch of flowers. So the professor explained the reasons for his apparently so severe judgment. With a piece of paper he covered part of the picture, leaving the viewer to guess what might be the age of the person of whom all that could be seen was a hand holding a bunch of flowers. It was a young girl's hand. But repeating the same procedure with different parts of the body, it seemed that the foot was that of an adult woman and the shoulders were even said to be a man's. In other words, each detail seemed beautiful, but it was not attuned with the person. In the same way, plans that are inconsistent with the personal vocation destroy the image of God of which the person him/herself is a bearer. In the novel *The Brothers Karamazov*, Ivan the rationalist ends up mad, with a double personality. How different is the outcome which led to the oft-repeated suggestion which Theophan the Recluse gave to his spiritual children: unite the head to the heart, think about the spiritual identity given by the Spirit which resides in the heart. Therefore the best spiritual fathers are those who possess knowledge of the heart. And that is why they can judge which are the thoughts to keep and which to be rejected.

10

So, to clearly distinguish the usefulness or harmfulness of thoughts one has to be aware of one's own identity?

Yes, but in the spiritual sense, that is identity understood as divine vocation. When one speaks of vocation in the «secular sense», it is understood as a work choice, a choice of place in society, choice about a way of living, a choice made at a mature age. But in the eyes of God our vocation precedes our existence. God creates human beings with their specific vocation in mind, the work to which they are called. Those who follow it faithfully, paint, so to speak, a perfect picture, an image of God in his perfection. The classic example has been given by the life of Mary Most Holy: pre-chosen to be the Mother of God, she followed throughout her life everything that corresponded to this call.

11

But how can one know one's own vocation?

An answer cannot be given in just a few words. But one can point to the fundamental principle from which other concrete applications follow: it is the voice of the pure heart which indicates the path which God has destined us to follow. The voices of evil which try to deviate us from this proposal come «from outside». Such a principle, obviously, needs to be further explained. We will do this gradually. It will be easier to describe first of all how a thought comes «from outside», in order to be able then to understand the inner voice of the heart.

The psychophysical method of the Hesychasts

1

Christian Yoga?

Today there are a few people —not just in the Far East, but in Europe, too— who practice yoga and claim it is an effective exercise for gaining peace of soul. The Congregation for the Doctrine of the Faith felt obliged to point out the dangers linked to it. It is clear that the faithful cannot accept any of the theories which often go along with yoga if these contradict Christian teaching. But that doesn't hold for yoga if it is practiced as a sort of gymnastic exercise which is very useful for someone who lives in the city and has more or less lost contact with natural life. Furthermore, someone in our technical society thinks of being able to exercise the body in various types of sporting activity independently from considering the soul and, inversely, believes it possible to dedicate oneself to the activities of the soul by forgetting and disdaining one's own body. In this regard, whoever practices yoga wishes to re-establish the unity lost between these two elements. It is clear that this has implications, too, in the area of prayer. When one prays intensely, the body's incorrect postures produce tiredness and neurosis. On the contrary, a correct physical position helps concentration in prayer. What practical conclusions can be drawn?

2

The body's peace

We must admit that, in the psychological considerations of the ancient Greek authors, just as in the language of the Christian ascetics, a weak point emerges: the negative attitude toward physical reality. Christians were unable to consider matter as evil. On the other hand, the ascetics always remained convinced that the body created by God remains, after sin, the sphere most exposed to the temptations of the devil. Renouncing the body is therefore a constant object of ascetic exhortation. But as regards the «use» of the body and its disposition in prayer there are only brief references in occasional notes.

From this point of view, therefore, the «physical method» of the Mount Athos monks in the 14th-15th centuries represents progress. The ancient Hesychasts of Egypt and Sinai did not doubt that peace of soul shone out through the face and pacified bodily passions. The physical method wishes to highlight the opposite aspect: peaceful exercise of the physical functions calms the soul and prepares it for prayer.

3
The Hesychast movement

For many contemporaries it was a discovery to realize that many of the yoga exercises were already practiced a few centuries ago by Christian monks. We have referred to those who lived on Mount Athos. They were part of a major current of Eastern spirituality called «Hesychasm». The Greek term *hesychia* means: calm, peace, rest, tranquility. From the outset, there were many «Hesychasts» among the Egyptian Desert Fathers who considered their own vocation to be dedicating themselves completely to prayer, with no concerns for anything else. They considered external and internal peace to be a necessary condition for such a life. Therefore they lived in solitude and practiced control of thoughts, «inner vigilance», understood as we have already explained.

Later this tendency was warmly welcomed on Mount Athos where, at the start of the 14th century, a Calabrian monk, Nicephorus, invented a «physical method» to facilitate prayer, using some body positions. In fact the re-awakening of this type of prayer took place thanks to the dissemination of the *Philocalia*, an anthology of texts from the Fathers and Hesychast authors collected by Macarios of Corinth (†1805) and Nicodemus of the Holy Mountain (†1809). Now such a work is also well known in the West. Furthermore, thanks to the numerous editions of *The Tales of a Russian Pilgrim*, the West has also got to know about the «Jesus Prayer», typical short prayer in the Hesychast method. It is through these publications that interest has increased in these methods which promise the acquisition of peace by means of a «physical method».

4
The Russian Pilgrim
∽

Let us begin with this rather late writing. It contains instruction on the physical method explained in a somewhat rudimentary fashion. The author is unknown. In 1881 four accounts were published in Kazan, in Russia, in which a devout pilgrim narrated his search for the acquisition of the gift of constant prayer, sought by repeating without pause the Jesus Prayer. Re-printed many times in Russian and translated into other languages, these tales have become not just one of the best-known works of spiritual literature, but also a source of great importance for the study of spirituality.

5
The «Russian Pilgrim's» method of constant prayer
∽

The method of this prayer can followed step by step in *The Tales.* The account begins by setting out the main problem in continuous prayer: how do you «pray constantly» (*1 Thess* 5:17)? The pilgrim meets one of the *starets*, that is a spiritual father, expert in the «Jesus Prayer». From him he receives the command to recite three thousand short prayers a day to gain the habit of reciting the Jesus Prayer orally, so that such repetition might become a spontaneous habit, even if still purely externally, a movement of the lips. Then the *starets* commanded him to recite six thousand prayers a day. The pilgrim barely succeeded in doing it, but subsequently practiced this repetition to such an extent that the habit continued from being just when awake to when asleep, too. The lips moved even when he was asleep.

The pilgrim was happy and began to believe that he had arrived at the state of constant prayer. But he took a new, further step. To hide the fact of praying in the presence of others, he stopped moving his lips and tried to say the prayers moving only his tongue. In the end he seemed to have got used to it. But the process did not end there. Prayer had to reach the stage where invoking Jesus had to be united with the heartbeat. Here is what he himself did and how, later on, he taught such a method to a blind person: «Imagine your heart, fix your eyes as if you were looking through the chest in as lively a manner as you can, and, with your ears pricked up, listen to how the heart beats, one beat after another. When you are used to it, try to adjust the words of the prayer to every heartbeat, without losing it from view. Or better, at the first beat say or think: «Lord», at the second «Jesus», at the third «Christ», at the fourth «have mercy», at the fifth «on me», and repeat it many times».

Linked to the beat of the heart, the prayer is, so to speak, inseparable from life itself. At least that is how the pilgrim understood it and thus found his happiness: «When someone insults me, I think only of the beneficial Jesus Prayer. Immediately anger or misery completely disappear. My spirit has become truly simple. I do not give myself up to any misery, nothing concerns me, nothing external detains me… When I am hit by a violent cold, I recite the prayer with greater attention and soon I feel warm and comforted. If hunger is too insistent, I invoke even more the name of Jesus Christ and I no longer recall having been hungry».

∽

The pilgrim's text is, as we have said, a late text. In addition, what is called the «physical method», that is the use of bodily means to achieve mental concentration, is only partially explained there. The complete traditional explanation is found in the work of the Athonite monk Nicephorus *On Vigilance and the Guarding of the heart*. The famous passage, taken up by the *Philocalia*, says: «Sit down in a calm cell, in some remote corner and do what I tell you: close the door, raise your spirit beyond every empty and temporal object. Then rest your beard on your chest and directing your bodily eye together with your entire intellect towards the middle of your belly, that is, towards your navel, restrain the inhalation of your breath through the nose, so as not to breathe in and out at your ease, and mentally search inwardly for the place of the heart, where reside the faculties of the soul. At the start you will find impenetrable darkness and thickness. But if you persevere, if you do this exercise day and night, then you will find, oh miracle!, an endless happiness. When the spirit finds the place of the heart, you will immediately see things never known before, you will see the heaven which exists in the midst of the heart, you will see yourself completely radiant, full of discernment. From this moment onwards, as soon as a [evil] thought arises, before it comes to completion and assumes a form, it will be put to flight by the invocation of the name of Jesus, which banishes and destroys it. From that moment the spirit, full of dislike of demons, will be inflamed with that anger which is second nature, that is to combat the spiritual enemies. The rest you will learn with God's help, when you will practice custody of the mind, keeping Jesus in the heart, because it was said: 'sit in the cell and all will be taught you'».

The symbolism of the body

In the method of the Russian pilgrim we have encountered in a practical manner two «physical» elements of prayer: the heartbeat and breathing.

From Nicephorus others must be noted: the position of the body (we note that in yoga it is the «position» of the body that matters, not movement, as in classical gymnastics), fixing attention on certain parts of the body (the heart, the navel), control of breathing, and an appropriate environment. These «physical» elements are directly associated with certain «psychic» effects: radiant visions (the Hesychasts speak of the «light of Tabor»), speediness of discernment, holy anger against the demons.

In this passage the followers of «Christian yoga» find various elements of support and are convinced that Nicephorus' method can be developed with the help of Indian or Japanese experiences. Up to what point can this path be pursued? We believe that it is important to set down a prior marker. It was correctly noted that the fundamental relationship with reality is different between the East and the West. Whatever happens, the West focuses its attention on discovering the relationship between cause and effect. The Eastern attitude is different. Faced with what happens, the Eastern approach is to ask: «What is the meaning of what we see? Of what hidden reality might it be the symbol?»

These two attitudes also exist when one speaks about the physical method of prayer. A Western observer would usually ask: «What effect does slowing down the breathing produce? And focusing attention on the heart?» Consequently, the physical method becomes, for Westerners, a sort of gymnastic culture adapted for contemplatives.

Eastern observers, on the other hand, see symbolism here, too, and ask: «What significance can be given to the heartbeat?

And breathing? And the feeling of warmth?» This was the attitude of the Fathers who defended the cult of sacred images and contemplation of visible nature. Such must be the attitude to assume with regard to the function of the body in prayer, so that the person praying, as Origen writes, «bears in the body the image of the soul's feelings». In short, one must be capable of also understanding the different bodily states and feelings as «images» of the spiritual state of the soul.

Up to a certain point we all do it. Joining our hands, kneeling down, bowing profoundly are all traditional signs of prayer. But why should symbolism end here? Can't we also give a symbolic and spiritual meaning to breathing, the heartbeat, concentrating on the heart? The advocates of the physical method are convinced that it is an effective method to achieve constant prayer, since in such a way it becomes associated with the vital functions which never stop. And it is under this aspect that we can consider the individual physical elements, so highly recommended by the Hesychasts, as suitable for prayer.

8

To sit in a humble position

The body, in a conscious or unconscious manner, takes part in the movements of the soul, the thoughts, desires, feelings and decisions. However there is a major difference between the movement of the body and its position. Movement is the symbol of an action which is taking place. For example, we raise the hand the say to others: «Listen to what I'm saying!» Position, on the other hand, is the sign of an on-going state. When we are sitting comfortably, then we are saying to others that we want to remain in that place. The body, forced to remain in a position, adjusts, who knows how, the nerves, muscles, and circulation to this state.

The ideal of Eastern prayer, and above all Hesychast prayer, is to attain a state (*katastasis*), a stable disposition of the heart, a «being simply with the Lord», to experience his presence. The person who sits in a humble position, by this gesture symbolizes and strengthens such a disposition and spontaneously repeats: «Lord, have mercy on me, a sinner!»

9
The closed cell, the low light

Closing the door of the room means that we want to be alone. The Hesychasts led an eremitic, solitary life. Therefore they often repeated the advice: «Remain in your cell, it will teach you everything!» So they wanted to receive instruction not from strangers, but from the inspiration which stems from the heart. It would therefore be wrong to believe that spiritual solitude arises simply from the absence of contact with other people. Even more important is the «solitude of the heart», which succeeds in eliminating the «discourses» produced by the thoughts which disturb. They are also caused by the different objects which we see around us. A scarcely lit room is an environment which loses shape and color. It therefore becomes an invitation to seek God beyond the images or ideas and experience him as a pure light which invades the heart.

10
Breathing

The regularity of breathing coordinated with prayer is a natural exercise for someone who desires nothing but to savor the words of the prayer in the rhythm of their own life. The terms «to breathe» and «to live» are also linguistically related in different languages. In Slav the word for «truth» (*istina*) originally means «what exists and breathes». The person who unites the name of Jesus with every breath wants to experience how the reality of Christ penetrates and gives life to all that exists. But the person who breathes normally feels the need to slow down the rhythm and even stop it. The spiritual life unfolds on earth and is at the same time eternal life. God is master of time and in union with him the human person tries to stop what is happening. Those who practice yoga say that the slowing down of breathing slows down life's biological rhythm and the ageing process. With this method the Christian can live the experience of «eschatological time»: he/she does not want to measure the course of life according to the clock, but according to the closeness of Christ.

Breathing comprises three phases: inhaling, holding breath, and breathing out. The person who inhales experiences dependency on the world. To unite this phase with the Jesus Prayer means experiencing dependence on Him, who is the Life of the world in the spiritual sense. Breathing out is the solace of the person who feels in full possession of the same life and desires to give it, distribute around him/herself.

11

To focus attention on the place of the heart

In yoga great importance is attached to the pinpointing of thought, uniting it with an organ to which it should correspond according to the person's psychophysical structure. It is presumed that different thoughts have their «natural seat» in specific organs. The Hesychasts state that prayer must be focused in the heart in a material sense, too, in the chest, slightly to the left.

An Eastern bishop —who was also a doctor—, advocate of the prayer of the heart, tried to make a summary of his studies on this problem. He distinguished four locations, believing that thought can be pinpointed 1) in the cerebrofrontal center; 2) the buccopharyngeal center; 3) in the pectoral center; and, 4) in the cardiac center.

The cerebrofrontal center is situated between the eyebrows. It corresponds to the abstract thought of pure intelligence. It can be a very intense, lucid thought, but also very unstable. Concentration of this kind needs great will power, which entails effort and the dissipation of energy.

In the buccopharyngeal center thought loses its abstract character and enters into the dynamism of life. But it is still unstable.

Thought situated in the pectoral center, in the middle of the chest, participates in respiration; it therefore acquires a more stable rhythm.

But a greater stability is acquired when the location is fixed right in the heart.

According to yoga, respiration is more united to «idea», while the heart is more united to «feeling». For Russian monks, the «feeling of the heart» speaks of a stable disposition, therefore a «state» of prayer. Hence the authors often advise: «Descend from the head into the heart!»

12

Warmth

Regulated breathing produces effects of warmth which from the chest spread out into the whole of the body and create a sense of joy. The pulse becomes stronger and could be accompanied by phenomena of radiant visions. But all the spiritual authors on these occasions strictly warn: these are natural effects, it is not grace! It would be a dangerous error to believe that it is a mystical experience. The value of these feelings depends on the use one makes of them for the good of prayer. Both warmth and light are images of the Holy Spirit. As images they can serve to help raise the mind toward the reality they represent. But to seek them for themselves alone would be pure idolatry.

13
Sense of peace and harmony

ॐ

If well-done the physical method produces calm attuning the various vital functions to the same rhythm: the heartbeat, respiration, walking, vocal prayer and the good thoughts that follow. All this makes one think of God's peace which is a messianic gift (cf. *Luke* 2:14; 19:38, etc.). But the sense of peace obtained by the physical method could easily degenerate into quietism, in which one lays claim to peace without any further goals. This harmony must instead be understood as the disposition of one who focuses all their strengths to better hear the voice of God and is pre-disposed to combat, as if they were in an inner castle, the «demons» which come «from outside».

14
Control of vital energy

ॐ

Well-regulated respiration enables, as yoga claims, bringing the amount of *prâna*, which the human person possesses, to its level of greatest intensity. So nutrition by external food is reduced to the minimum. Christian Hesychasts, too, are persuaded that the physical method presumes the practice of fasting, sometimes very rigorous, but at the same time joyful, accompanied by a sense of inner freedom with respect to the needs of the body. How many examples of that can be found in the biographies of the monastic saints!

15

The dangers to avoid

༜ᕲ

The insistence with which some Christian authors allowed the practice of the physical method only under the supervision of an expert spiritual father perhaps seem exaggerated. Why so many precautions? The method is simple! One person who was preoccupied about the matter and wrote to the Russian bishop Ignatius Brjan aninov received the reply: «The method is simple, but you aren't!» Not everyone is equally capable of living and deepening the symbolism, not all are capable of moving from the sign to the spiritual reality that is being sought. It happens here just as with icons: to stop without moving beyond means making of the image an idol, of the path an obstacle in the raising of the mind to God. To see one's own body as a spiritual symbol is yet more difficult, because it could degenerate into worship of the body and carnal feelings. Certain «physical» exercises almost automatically produce feelings which resemble the spiritual consolations: calm, the joy of being alone, phenomena of light and warmth. To confuse them with the true spiritual consolations would be one of the deviations most feared by spiritual authors and to strive to give them a mystical significance, when the life of the human person is not at such a level, is a type of schizophrenia which leads to mental aberrations.

16

A practical note

༜ᕲ

However, one must not exaggerate the precautions, either. Something simple can be attempted even alone. For example, we find ourselves in a tranquil environment. The right hand takes the left to feel the rhythm of the pulse. We try to attune breathing or walking to the same rhythm. When we have succeeded, we repeat a brief ejaculatory prayer suitable to our state of soul, to the feelings which dominate us. Praying in this way for some time, the experience will teach us how to benefit from this peaceful state to make the dialog with God the Father more intense.

In this way, prayer is greatly simplified, but on the other hand all our being, soul and body is involved. This the human person feels united in him/herself and with God. Today's technical culture has become extremely «analytical». Therefore, the human person in his/her subconscious feels attracted by what helps them to live in their own integrity, so as to arrive, at certain times, «at a state in which, in the mortal body, one possesses an image of eternal happiness» (Cassian).

Praying «in the heart»

1
Raising of the mind or heart?

The traditional definition of prayer states that it is «the raising of the mind to God». Its origin goes back to Plato. Christian authors adopted it, but also interpreted it so that it became more complete. It is not just the mind that is active in prayer, but the whole person, even if the decisive role belongs to the soul. We can distinguish three faculties in it: the intellect, the will, and the heart. Each of these three «faculties» can be more or less dominant in the different types of prayer. We know about intellective, reflective prayer. Prayer «sets in motion» what is realized starting from a decision of the will which formulates good propositions. But, according to authors from the Christian East, the more perfect prayer is that in which the «feelings of the heart» predominate. For example, Theophan the Recluse writes: «When you speak your prayer, try to do it in a way that it comes from the heart. In its true sense, prayer is nothing but a breath of the heart toward God; when this impulse is missing, you cannot talk of prayer».

2
A danger of sentimentalism?

If not dangerous, it seems almost banal to say that real prayer and religion must above cultivate the «feelings of the heart». The prudent person reflects and decides according to sound reason. Feelings are secondary and very changeable reactions. In fact the Church condemned the maxim of the «Modernists» in the last century which stated that religiosity should have its origin in the subconscious, in irrational sentiments. To respond to this serious objection, it is necessary to clarify very well what is understood by the concept of heart and its sentiments.

3

The heart in the Bible

Modern language distinguishes three different activities of our soul: to think, to desire, and to feel. Therefore we have three separate faculties: the intellect, the will and the heart. This terminology cannot be applied to biblical texts, where such psychological distinctions are not made. There people speak spontaneously, in a similar way to how simple people speak today, too. One can observe the human person externally, as can be seen in the body. But everyone knows that the person's inner value can be different. For example, a person can speak in a charitable manner, but in his/her heart nourish hatred. With the term «heart» we mean everything to do with a person's inner life. So in the Bible, too, it is said that someone reflects, decides, reacts in secret «in his/her heart». When someone preserves something in the heart, it means it cannot be forgotten. In conclusion: the heart, in these texts, does not mean one of the soul's faculties, but the whole person, in the integrity of all their faculties and fundamental attitude toward people, God and the world. When the Scripture says we must love God «with all one's heart», it means «with all your soul and with all your mind» (*Matt* 22:37), «with all your strength» (*Mark* 12:30; *Luke* 10:27).

This human integrity can be considered under a dual aspect: one «static», the other «dynamic». Obviously, that has to be explained. Remember our common experience. For example, a young person loves his girlfriend with all his heart, experiences no contrary sentiment, and freely decides to marry her. Such is his disposition today. Will it be the same tomorrow? We are not sure. This attitude of today, the disposition of the present moment, we call «static». Subsequently the young man marries his girlfriend and as husband is faithful to her and loves her forever. This stable disposition, lasting through all the vicissitudes of life, we call «dynamic».

4
Human integrity considered in a «static» manner

We will try to explain it further with help of a concrete example. I am very busy, because I have to finish an urgent piece of work. Unfortunately, an inconvenient visitor comes to see me. What must I do? Should I rudely send him away? I know he would be saddened by this. So I decide to make a sacrifice and I welcome him with a courtesy freely chosen, but forced. When this is done stimulated by charity, one is certainly performing a worthy task. Life forces us to make such sacrifices. But we sense that they are not entirely normal actions since, within us, there is division. We do good, but not «with all one's heart». The ideal is knowing how to overcome these divisions and act in a spontaneous way, «with all one's soul».

5
The prayer of the heart under the «static» aspect

How many times are we divided within during prayer! With goodwill we pick up the Psalter to recite the Psalms. But the intellect flies and many disparate thoughts come to mind. And what can be said about feelings? We pray for the salvation of our neighbor, but at the same time we feel antipathy toward him. How wonderful it would be to pray with all one's heart! Spiritual authors are convinced that such an ideal of prayer can be attained. The different «methods of meditation» are nothing but an exercise in this area. We recall the method of Ignatian meditation, where many elements are recommended: putting oneself in the presence of God, choosing the body's position suitable for prayer, picturing oneself in the place (for example, when we meditate on the Christmas mystery, the stable where Jesus was born), reflecting on the meaning of the words of the gospel or the text of the prayer, deciding what conclusions will ensue for our lives, doing it with complete love and asking for God's grace with the intercession of the saints. One notes that different aspects of our life are exposed in an analytical manner, but the aim is that in prayer all will be united. So the whole person is praying, with great intensity and with great peace.

6

The prayer of the heart under the «dynamic» aspect

The heart under the «dynamic» aspect signifies the unity of the person in the course of life. What am I? What I decided yesterday or what awaits me tomorrow? As it is «in the heart», so it is normally, always, not just in the present, but at whatever specific instant. Prayer, in this sense, signifies a stable, lasting disposition. Such prayer is by its nature continuous, inseparable from the person. The best example of this state is described to us in the biography of Saint Francis of Assisi, where one reads: «His whole intuition and all his affection was addressed to the Lord… so (from what one can say) he was not so much a man who prays, but rather he himself was completely transformed into a living prayer». In this sense, Saint Thomas Aquinas also defined devotion as the «inclination of the will to every good». Doubtless, this is also how one must interpret the text in the Ignatian meditation entreating that «love» be added to the rational reflections and concrete propositions of the will. Of course, this does not signify some banal feeling, but the effort undertaken so that the meditated truth becomes our normal mentality. So just as we expect a true lover of music to play his/her instrument at every occasion that lends itself to the opportunity, so in the same way we expect that the person who is humble of heart manifests this attitude in every circumstance. And whoever has acquired the habit of prayer in the heart raises his/her spirit to God at every moment.

7

How can we bw aware of the state of the heart?

This is both an old and always current problem. Moral textbooks help us to distinguish individual acts and we can therefore judge their value: to steal is evil, to give to charity is good, etc. A confessor, even if we are seeing them for the first time, can tell us, judging according to the traditional criteria, if in a concrete case we have acted well or badly. However, he keeps silent when I pose the question: «How am I in the sight of God? What is my state with regard to eternity?» The heart remains a mystery, it is the hidden part of the human person, that which only God knows. On the other hand, the person, too, must know him/herself, measure their progress in spiritual life. It can be done, the authors assure us that the soul is very clear-minded and the human person, depending on the level of his/her own innocence and inner purity, has a direct self-intuition.

According to Theophan the Recluse, the notion of heart includes this form of integral and intuitive self-knowledge. This is about the «feelings of the heart». «The function of the heart consists in feeling everything which touches upon our person». Obviously, not all «feelings» have the same value. Their infallibility and usefulness for the spiritual life will depend on the purity of the heart itself.

8

The heart —source of revelation

Therefore the heart has a voice which makes itself heard. The same Theophan writes: «Consequently, always and continually, the heart feels the state of the soul and body, as well as the multiform impressions produced by particular actions, spiritual and physical, the objects which surround us or which we come up against us, our external situation and, in general, the course of our life». We see and think many things, but only the heart tells us what value they have for life.

The heart ensures the correctness of faith. Believers are not able to prove their faith in Christ by arguments of reason. But the feeling of the heart gives them the certainty of being on the right path of salvation: «Everybody who believes in the Son of God has this testimony inside him» (1 John 5:10).

The pure heart also makes us know others. The famous spiritual fathers, like the Russian *startsi*, were surprising in their knowledge of hearts. It was said of Saint Seraphim of Sarov that he read people's hearts like an open book. It is interesting that this was not considered to be a miraculous gift. God has created us, they used to say, so that we should know each other. Sin constitutes a wall between people. For the person who attains purity of heart, the hearts of others are open. Therefore, given that the heart is purified above all by love, only the person who loves the other can understand it.

9

The pure heart fount of contemplation of God

«To see God in all things» —with these words Eastern authors define Christian contemplation. It is a high ideal, but on the other hand it is a program for all Christians. Rightly, however, we ask how we can get there. The word contemplation, in Greek *theoria*, means «to see», and every person desires to see the reality with which they come into contact. However there are different ways of seeing. The first is with the eyes. In such a way one cannot see God, since He is invisible. Our intellect, which formulates clear ideas and abstract principles, offers us a superior vision. But not even along this path does one arrive at God, since He exceeds all human intellect. And yet Christ has promised us the vision of God: «Happy the pure in heart: they shall see God» (*Matt* 5:8).

A Syriac mystic, Martyrius Sahdônâ, wrote: «Ah, the clear eye of the heart which sees in the open, thanks to its purity, the One at whose sight the seraphim cover their faces! Where, therefore, will [God] be loved if not in the heart? And where will he manifest himself, if not there? Blessed are the pure in heart because they will see God».

Given that the pure heart is the one that loves, says correctly a recent Eastern author, this expression of Leonardo da Vinci is prophetic with regard to any modern intellectualism: «Great love springs from great knowledge», one loves the beauty he/she has known. And yet we Christians can say the opposite: «Great knowledge springs from great love». «God is love» (*1 John* 4:8). Without charity it is therefore impossible to know him.

10
The heart knows God by means of inner inspiration

We have seen that the human person is often overrun by a multitude of thoughts. To judge their usefulness for life, it is necessary to examine not just what they say, but also where they come from. Under this aspect, the Fathers try first of all to distinguish if they come «from outside» or «from within». The thoughts that come to us from outside have many different sources: we have seen something which makes us think, heard a story, a speaker who has «suggested» an idea to us. The spiritual authors experienced that the devil, too, suggests various ideas to destroy us. On the other hand, we are convinced that God also speaks to us through inspirations. The Holy Spirit in fact suggests ideas to us. But his way of drawing close to us is different to that of the enemy, his voice, in fact, makes itself heard «from within».

The Syriac authors describe this experience with a metaphor. The heart, they say, is like a fountain. If it is pure, the sky is reflected in it. Likewise in the pure heart divine thoughts are reflected. Whoever is used to experiencing them, has no need of other teachings. The authors call «prayer of the heart» listening to the divine inspirations within oneself.

11

Prayer of the heart described by Western Saints

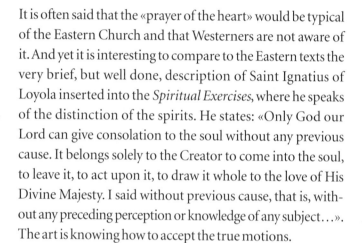

It is often said that the «prayer of the heart» would be typical of the Eastern Church and that Westerners are not aware of it. And yet it is interesting to compare to the Eastern texts the very brief, but well done, description of Saint Ignatius of Loyola inserted into the *Spiritual Exercises*, where he speaks of the distinction of the spirits. He states: «Only God our Lord can give consolation to the soul without any previous cause. It belongs solely to the Creator to come into the soul, to leave it, to act upon it, to draw it whole to the love of His Divine Majesty. I said without previous cause, that is, without any preceding perception or knowledge of any subject…». The art is knowing how to accept the true motions.

In the ancient biography of Saint Francis one reads that very often he had such intuitions and he did not let himself escape them. On the contrary, he accepted them with great care. Thus, when he was walking with others, if an «enlightenment» came to him, he let the others go on ahead and he stopped to listen to this voice of the Lord. Again it is said that, at these moments, he placed a hand on his heart (a gesture which became recommended by the Hesychasts) «and there spoke with the Lord, there responded to his judge, there entreated his Father, conversed with his Friend, gratified [his soul] with his Bridegroom».

12
Knowing oneself by knowing God

Christian thought has taken up and the developed the motto carved on the Temple at Delphi, handed down to us by Socrates: «Know yourself!» But for Christian authors what exactly does know yourself mean? It is not psychological knowledge, but rather what is called «moral»: knowing what good we are capable of achieving, what virtues we must practice. But Saint Basil speaks of a self-knowledge yet more sublime, «theological»: to know God, contemplating his image in our soul and listening to the voice of the Spirit in one's heart. It is this latter which is carried out in the so-called «prayer of the heart».

13
The reality of prayer of the heart

As regards this prayer «of the heart», it is often said that it would be a privilege of Eastern ascetics, while Westerners would not be aware of it.

It is true that Easterners talk about it a lot. The Russian theologian B Vyšeslavcev writes: «If religion is a personal relationship with God, then contact with the Divinity is only possible in the depths of my «I», in the depths of the heart, because God, as Pascal says, is perceptible to the heart». And yet, the surprising thing, one of the best descriptions, even very short, of this prayer is to be found in the text already quoted of Saint Ignatius of Loyola about thoughts and attitudes which do not have «an external cause». We live in a technical society and we are used to thinking that everything that happens has an external cause, every movement an impetus from another force. The positivist psychologists have taught us that a child's soul is a *tabula rasa*, in which we will find only what other people will write there. Therefore society tries to «indoctrinate us», in the good and bad senses of the word. Therefore, the human person is used to listening only to others, no longer pays attention to the inspirations of the heart, which come from the Spirit. It is a privilege of artists to have «inspirations», but not exclusively. In the spiritual life everyone must be an «artist» and construct their own life under the guidance of the supreme «Artist». «The pure of heart», states Saint Francis of Assisi, «are those who despise earthly things and seek the things of heaven, and who never cease to adore and behold the Lord God living and true with a pure heart and soul».

Epilogue

1
Paul Claudel: the heart

«During a concert, who would not have followed with appreciation and approval the gestures of the conductor of the orchestra? (And perhaps to really enjoy it completely it would be better to be deaf!). The people of his subordinates are in rows before us, one row after another, each absolutely obedient to his every silent whisper. But we, unfortunately, only see his back, we cannot benefit from his anxious glance, desperate or triumphant, severe, pleading, insistent, threatening, persuasive, the look which moves from the violins to the double basses to the trumpets. His right hand holds like a shaft of lightning the bow which plays the human instrument, while the left hand, imperious or benedictory, with the five fingers open and the palm soft and vibrant, caresses, like hair, like the coat of a poorly domesticated dog, the intelligent and manifold animal which listens to him, and from his protégée he makes the sound come forth. The right hand provides the standard with authority and sweetness, but the left hand, in most varied details, provides the feeling. It arouses the touch».

This happens, too, in the spiritual structure within us. There is a conductor of our «organic machine», which indicates the standard, but at the same time shapes within us, expresses and qualifies the feeling. It is the heart, this learned and complicated instrument, furnished with many keys, vents and shelves. It is called to direct within us an organic orchestra, to provide the measure of life. It beats, but at the same time it listens. It is not by chance that its upper parts have been given the name «auricle». In Adam, it received the lasting and constant impetus from the Breath of the mouth of the Eternal One. But not content with that, he continues to give new impulses…

«Inveni cor meum!» says the Prophet. I have found my heart! What a discovery! Nothing less than my heart! Noth-

ing less than the essence of my person. Something which existed before me, something in my chest which continues the beat of Adam. Something which knows more than I do and asks to be questioned in a manner different from words. Something which in our midst in entrusted with the care of being, which is interested in and responds to being. Something which we compare to a burning Bush, that Bush which burns without being consumed…

When the Master says: «Give me your heart!», that means: «My child, give me what is the center of yourself, your source, the regulating principle of your life, your perceptible, loving and intelligible rhythm. Reach your source! Beat together with Me!».

The art of purifying the heart

This book was printed on *thin opaque smooth white Bible paper*, using the *Minion* and *Type Embellishments One* font families.

This edition was printed in D'VINNI, S.A., in Bogotá, Colombia, during the last weeks of the fourth month of year two thousand ten.

Ad publicam lucem datus mensis aprilis, festivitatem Divina Misericordia